BUILT FOR SUCCESS

THE STORY OF

Published by Creative Education
P.O. Box 227, Mankato, Minnesota 56002
Creative Education is an imprint of The Creative Company.

DESIGN AND PRODUCTION BY **ZENO DESIGN**

Printed in the United States of America

PHOTOGRAPHS BY Alamy (David R. Frazier Photolibrary Inc.,
Bob Elam, Michael Gottschlak/AFP, Alex Segre, vario images
GmbH & Co.KG), Corbis (PETER MORGAN/Reuters, Kim
Kulish, Roger Ressmeyer, Ramin Talaie), Getty Images (TONY
AVELAR/AFP, FREDERIC J. BROWN/AFP, MARTIN BUREAU/
AFP, MICHAEL GOTTSCHALK/AFP, NASDAQ, Ralph Orlowski,
Panoramic Images, Mike Powell, Dick Strick/Time & Life
Pictures, Justin Sullivan)

LIBRARY OF CONGRESS CATALOGING-IN-PUBLICATION DATA

Gilbert, Sara.
The story of Google / by Sara Gilbert.
p. cm. — (Built for success)
Includes index
ISBN-13: 978-1-58341-605-1
1. Google (firm)—Juvenile literature. 2. Internet industry—
United States—Juvenile literature. I. Title.

HD9696.8U64G664 2008
338.7'6102504—dc22   2007014991

First edition

9 8 7 6 5 4 3 2 1

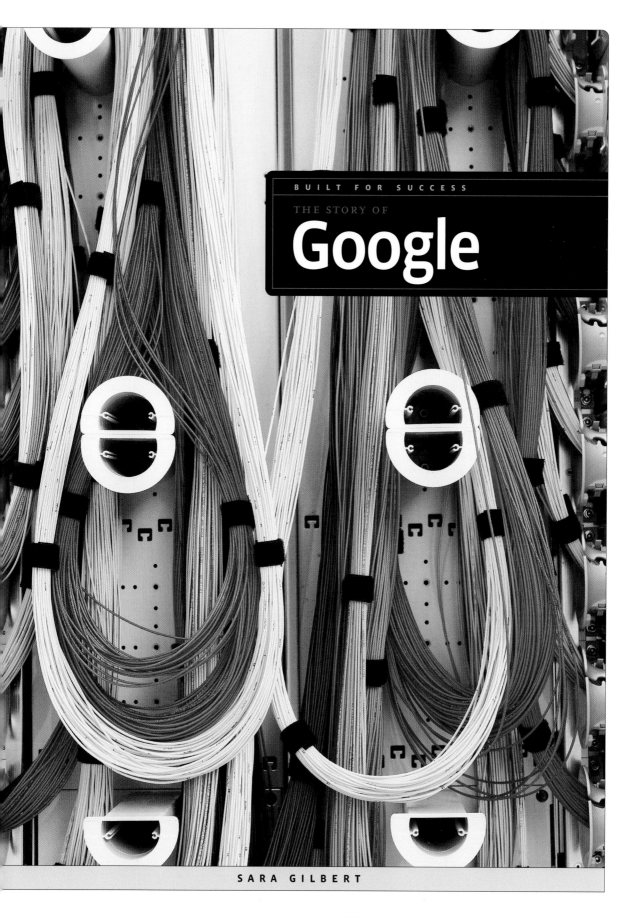

BUILT FOR SUCCESS

THE STORY OF

Google

SARA GILBERT

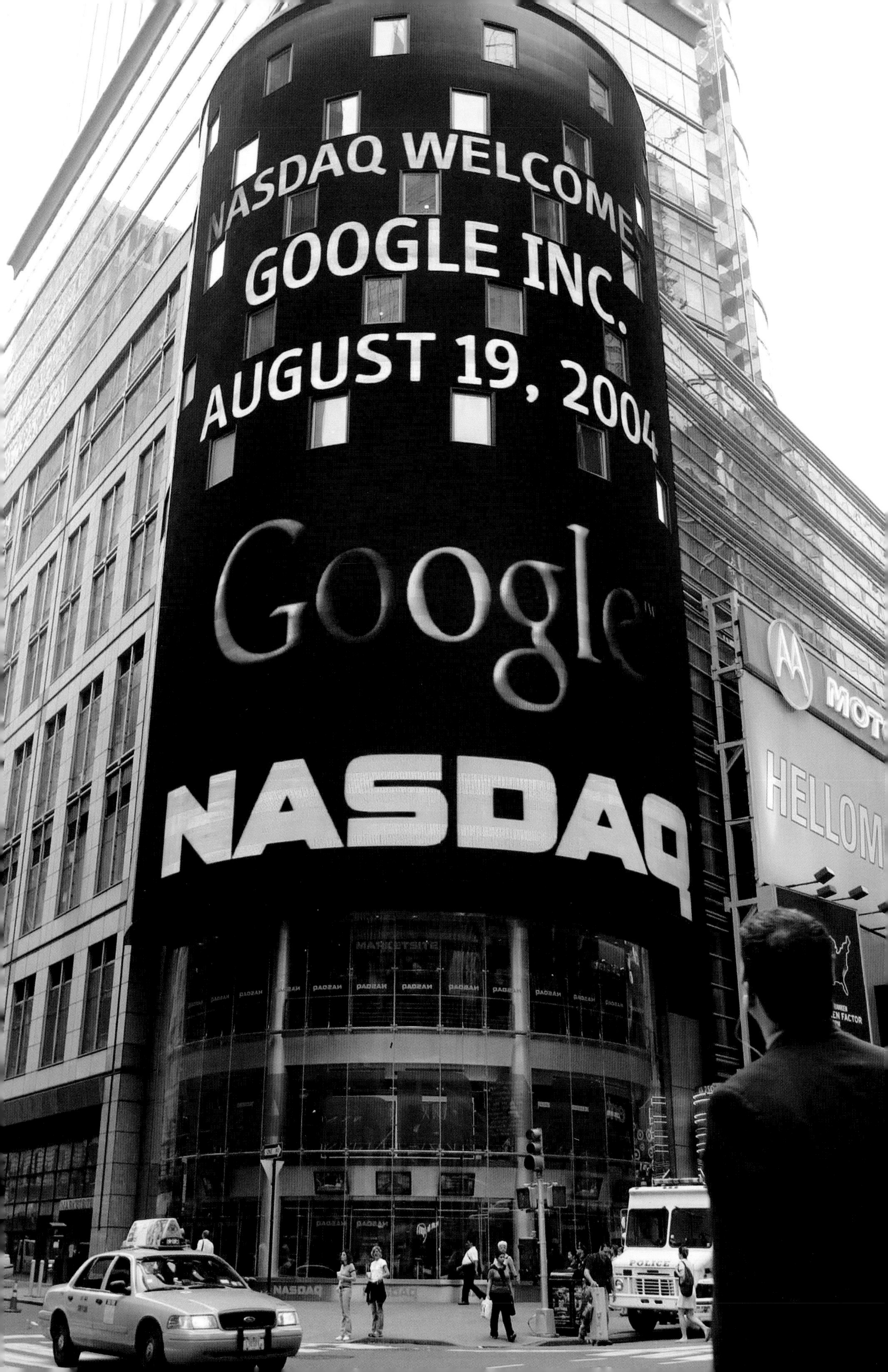
NASDAQ WELCOME
GOOGLE INC.
AUGUST 19, 2004
Google
NASDAQ

On August 19, 2004, at 9:30 A.M., Larry Page rang the opening bell at the NASDAQ Stock Market in New York City. Hours later, the 31-year-old Page and his partner, 30-year-old Sergey Brin, were multimillionaires. By the time the closing bell rang, Google, the Internet search engine the two friends had founded six years earlier, had sold $1.67 billion worth of stock in their company—and the young entrepreneurs were understandably excited. Their search engine was used by thousands of people searching for information on the World Wide Web and had already earned a global reputation as the leader in search technology. But now Google was also a public company flush with investors' dollars. And for Page and Brin, that just meant more money for more innovations.

CHAPTER ONE

A Stanford Start

Larry Page was in Palo Alto, California, visiting the campus of Stanford University, which had just accepted him into its prestigious PhD program in computer science, when he met Sergey Brin in the spring of 1995. Although Brin was only 23, a year younger than Page, he had already been in Stanford's graduate program for two years and was asked to help show Page around the university. Almost immediately, the two men—both bright, inquisitive, and up for a good-natured argument—hit it off.

That friendship blossomed when Page returned to Stanford the following fall. Almost as soon as they moved into the brand-new William Gates Computer Science building—named for the chairman of the Microsoft software company, who had donated $6 million for its construction— with the rest of the computer science students and faculty, they began working together on a project to download the entire World Wide Web and figure out a way to search it using **links** as a possible **doctoral thesis**. Page had decided that the number of links pointing to a particular site was an indicator of that site's popularity and relevance. He called his system of ranking pages through links "PageRank," a play on his own name.

Stanford University has an enrollment of more than 14,000 and a reputation as an elite school

By early 1997, PageRank had paved the way for a search engine called BackRub. Its first logo was a black-and-white scanned image of Page's left hand; when the duo decided to rename the search engine Google, they again opted for an inexpensive logo: the word spelled out in primary colors against a stark white background. "If you went to a design firm and asked for a homepage for a search engine, you would never get that," said Stanford professor Dennis Allison. "It doesn't have any animation or metallic colors, and there is no sound or lights. It flies completely in the face of the common belief that people love to find their way through the noise."

Allison was one of many in the Stanford community who caught on to the Google phenomenon in 1997, when the search engine was made available to students, faculty, and administrators at www.google.stanford.edu. Now that Brin and Page had users accessing their growing database, they needed more **hardware** to store all the information they were searching. But as graduate students, they had no budget for new **hard drives**. So they bought inexpensive parts, built their own machines, and hung around the loading docks on campus, looking for unclaimed computers that they could "borrow." They even maxed out their credit cards buying an exceptionally large amount of storage on disks. When they ran out of space in the office they shared with other graduate students, they turned Page's dorm room into a data center.

The two young men couldn't continue running their search engine on a shoestring budget. The ideal solution, they decided, was to license their search technology to an existing company. It was 1998, and the frenzy of emerging technology companies made for several potential partners. But all of the contacts they made with Internet companies such as AltaVista, Excite, and Yahoo! turned into dead ends. Most companies seemed more interested in making money on advertising than in improving their search engines.

The lack of outside enthusiasm for their product only made Brin and Page more determined to improve it. They sent letters to family and friends,

The Internet was expanding rapidly in the late 1990s as Larry Page and Sergey Brin built their search engine

encouraging them to use the search engine and asking for suggestions on ways to improve it. They asked everyone they knew to spread the word about the site. And they constantly tweaked the way Google looked and worked, including adding short summaries for each search result so that users could immediately see which results were most relevant to them.

By late summer of 1998, Brin and Page's database included 24 million Web pages—and it was still growing. But their funding was not. Then, one of their professors arranged a meeting with Andy Bechtolsheim, cofounder of Sun Microsystems and vice president of Cisco Systems, who had already made generous investments in a string of successful **start-ups**. In August 1998, Bechtolsheim visited with Brin and Page, who explained what they were working on and ran a demo for him, then discussed how they thought Google could actually make money by licensing their search technology to other Internet companies or even selling their ideas to a large company. Bechtolsheim was impressed. "This is the single best idea I have heard in years," he said. "I want to be part of this."

His part turned out to be a $100,000 check, written out on the spot to Google, Inc.—a company that, at the time, didn't even exist. Page had to tuck that check into his desk drawer until he and Brin had actually **incorporated** the company and opened a bank account on September 7, 1998. But for the moment, they decided to celebrate with breakfast at Burger King. Bechtolsheim, meanwhile, drove off wondering what would become of his investment. "In the back of my mind, I thought maybe they could get millions of people searching and add it all up and make money," he said later. "I didn't know how big this could be at the time. Nobody knew."

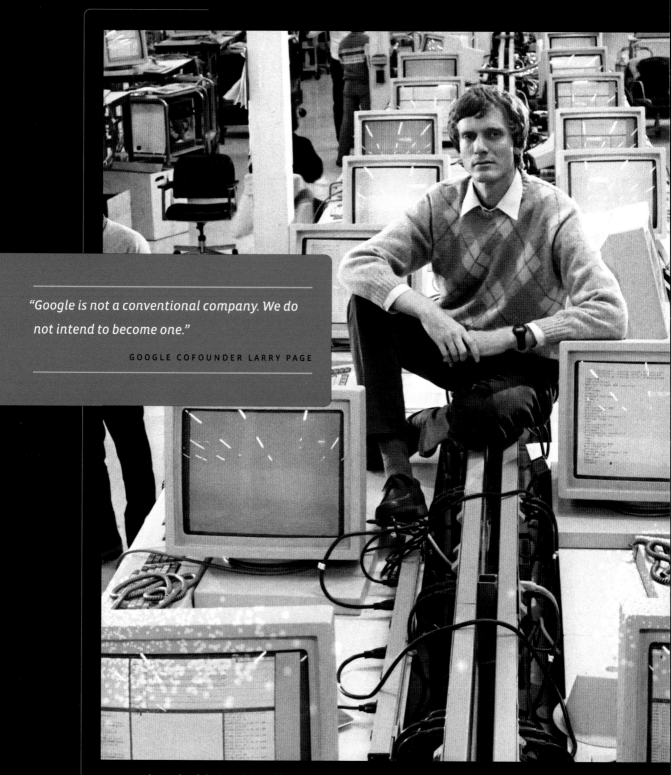

"Google is not a conventional company. We do not intend to become one."

GOOGLE COFOUNDER LARRY PAGE

Andy Bechtolsheim—himself a Stanford graduate—was among the first to see Google's potential

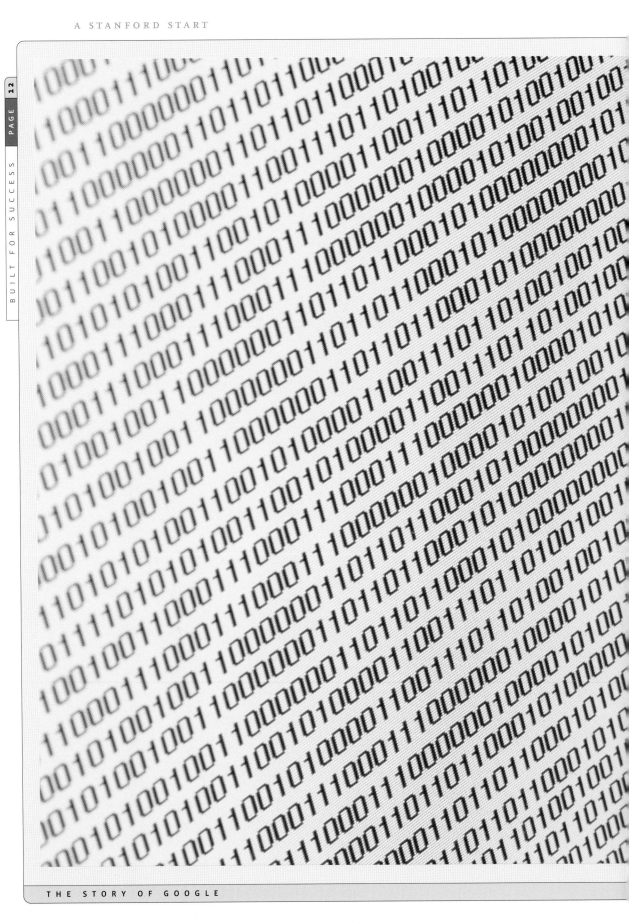

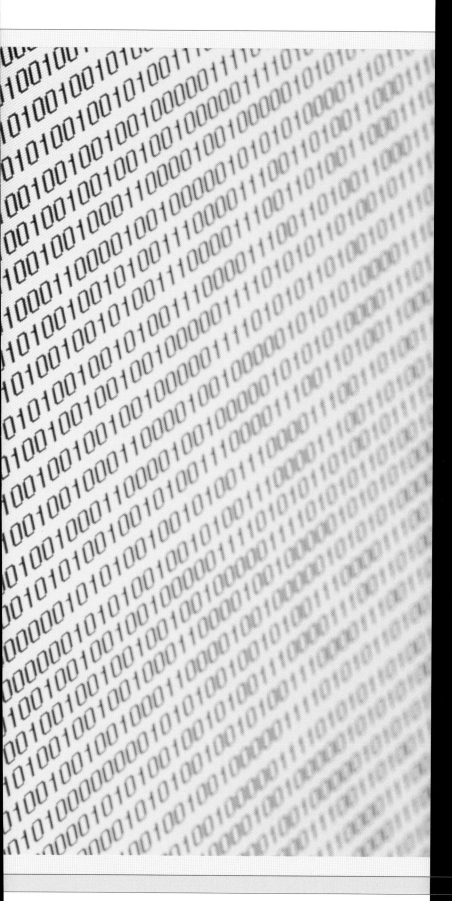

A NAME OF NUMBERS

Google's name is actually the result of an innocent misspelling that came out of days of brainstorming at Stanford. Larry Page and Sergey Brin had rejected idea after idea when Sean Anderson, a fellow graduate student, suggested "googleplex"—which is actually spelled "googolplex" and means the number 10 raised to the power googol—which represents the number 1 followed by 100 zeros. "You're trying to come up with a company that searches and indexes and allows people to organize vast amounts of data," Anderson explained. "Googleplex is a huge number." Larry Page suggested shortening it to Google, meaning the number 10 raised to the power 100. A quick check revealed that it was still available as a domain name, so they registered the name and scrawled it on a whiteboard in the office: google.com. But the next morning, another office mate left a note for them: "You misspelled it. It is supposed to be G-o-o-g-o-l."

CHAPTER TWO

The Little Engine That Could

The first official Google office was in a garage in Menlo Park, California, that Page and Brin, who had abandoned their studies at Stanford in 1998 to focus on their new business, rented from a friend for $1,700 a month. They enjoyed the perks of their new site, including use of the washer and dryer and occasional dips in the hot tub at their friend's house.

But after just five months, they had outgrown the garage. In early 1999, Google and its eight employees, all working to improve the software that by then was handling almost 500,000 search queries a day, took up residence in an office in downtown Palo Alto.

By then, Google.com had been mentioned in magazine articles and newspaper features and had been named a "Top 100 Web Site and Search Engine for 1998" by *PC Magazine*. It had even secured a client: Red Hat, a software firm that licensed the search technology. But it was running out of money, which was necessary to keep expanding the search technology and the company's capabilities. Page and Brin decided to seek out a **venture capital** firm for funding.

After researching their options, Page and Brin approached two of the most established firms in Silicon Valley, an area near San Francisco where many

This photo shows the Menlo Park garage that served as Google's headquarters in 1998 and 1999.

high-technology companies are based, hoping to secure financing from both. The young men impressed them not only with their technology and their long-term plans but also with their enthusiasm and friendly personalities. By the spring of 1999, both firms—Kleiner Perkins Caufield & Byers, and Sequoia Capital—were ready to invest a total of $25 million in Google. But neither one wanted to share the investment. Brin and Page were concerned that if they accepted funds from just one investor, they would lose control over their company. Although it was risky, they told both firms that the deal was off if they couldn't find a way to work together.

Neither firm wanted to lose out on what looked like a promising investment. So they decided to work together. Each company would invest $12.5 million in Google, and each would have a seat on the company's **board of directors**, but Page and Brin would maintain majority control. The only condition was that the young entrepreneurs had to hire a seasoned **executive** to run the business side of things. Page and Brin could see the value of that, and they agreed.

The influx of cash allowed Google's founders to aggressively recruit top people to their company. They had already put out feelers to their friends in the industry, promising that new employees would get **stock options**, free snacks and drinks at work, and the satisfaction of knowing that millions of people were using and appreciating the software that they would have a hand in developing. Now they could pay them as well.

But as Google hired more people and bought more computers, it ran short on space. The Palo Alto office became so cramped that employees couldn't get up from their desks without asking others to tuck their chairs in first. So, in late 1999, just as the tremendous interest in Internet companies was beginning to slow down, forcing many other technology businesses into bankruptcy, Google moved to a spacious new office in Mountain View, California.

As 1999 came to a close, Google was averaging a remarkable seven million searches a day—but Brin and Page still hadn't found a way to convert those

Located just south of San Francisco, Silicon Valley is home to many of the world's top computer businesses.

searches into a revenue stream. Although selling ads was the obvious choice, they worried that allowing advertising on their site would conflict with the motto they had established for their company, hoping to differentiate it from other companies driven purely by profits: Don't Be Evil. Search results, they believed, should always be free and unaffected by advertising. But they also were beginning to see the value of selling targeted ads that could accompany search results.

The solution they agreed upon was to sell Sponsored Links, a column of text-only links that ran on the right-hand side of the results page. The ads, like the search results, were displayed based on relevance, using a formula that balanced how much an advertiser was willing to pay (ads were sold in an auction format, with a "per-click" price that started at 5 cents a click) with how many times the ad was clicked on; the more popular ads were sent to the top of the page.

By the middle of 2000, the ads had turned into a solid revenue stream for Google. But more important to Brin and Page was the announcement in June of a partnership with Yahoo! to provide the huge Internet company with search results. Not only did that relationship expand Google's online exposure by millions of computer users, it also brought a certain credibility to its product.

The same week, Google announced that its index of Web sites had grown to include more than a billion pages, making it the world's largest search engine—not to mention the fastest and most relevant. "Now you can search the equivalent of a stack of paper more than 70 miles (113 km) high in less than half a second," Page said. "We think that's pretty cool."

> *"Don't be afraid of failure. The more you stumble around, the more likely you are to stumble across something valuable. And go into computer science only if you love it, not for the money."*
>
> GOOGLE COFOUNDER SERGEY BRIN'S ADVICE TO STUDENTS

By the year 2000, Google's huge yet seemingly simple search engine was gaining droves of users

goof-up ▶ n. informal a stupid mistake.

goof-us /ˈgoofəs/ ▶ n. informal a foolish or stupid person (often used as a general term of abuse). ⚠ based on GOOF.

goof-y /ˈgoofē/ ▶ adj. (goof-i-er, goof-i-est) informal 1 foolish; harmlessly eccentric. 2 (in surfing and other board sports) with the right leg in front of the left on the board. —goof-i-ly /-fəlē/ adv. —goof-i-ness n.

goo-gle /ˈgoogəl/ (also Google) ▶ v. informal [trans.] use an Internet search engine, particularly Google.com: she spent the afternoon googling aimlessly. ■ [trans.] search for the name of (someone) on the Internet to find out information about them: you meet someone, swap numbers, fix a date, then Google them through 1,346,966,000 Web pages. ▶ from Google, the proprietary name of a popular Internet search engine.

Google's founders never considered their company's name anything more than a noun meaning a very large number and representing the enormous size of their indexes. But users of the search engine quickly turned the name into a verb: People "googled" restaurants, schools, and even classmates, prospective employers, and dates. In 2006, a pair of dictionary publishers made that transition official. *Merriam-Webster* defined "google" as a transitive verb meaning "to use the Google search engine to obtain information about (a person) on the World Wide Web." The *Oxford English Dictionary* likewise included it as a verb, but listed it as "Google," capitalized. "A noun turns into a verb very often," explained Thomas Pitoniak, the associate editor and composition manager for *Merriam-Webster*. "Google is a unique case. Because they have achieved so much prominence in the world of search, people have been using the word google as a generic verb now."

CHAPTER THREE

Google Grows

In less than three years, Google had experienced incredible growth. By the beginning of 2001, it was handling more than 100 million search queries a day—about 10,000 a second—and had set out to make those searches better and more convenient by establishing relationships with several wireless Internet providers to make its technology available over cell phones and other devices. By the fourth **quarter**, it had recorded its first annual profit of $7 million.

But Page and Brin were delinquent on a promise they had made to their investors: They had not yet hired a chief executive officer (CEO) to run the business. Although John Doerr, a partner with the investment firm Kleiner Perkins, had arranged for several candidates to meet with them, the Google founders had seen reasons to reject all of them. When Eric Schmidt, a former chief technology officer for Sun Microsystems, came to Google's offices in late 2000, they expected to reject him as well. Schmidt, who was in the process of coordinating a **merger** for his new company, software-maker Novell, wasn't all that interested in their search engine or their job offer. But the meeting surprised both parties.

Starting around the year 2000, Google focused on making its technology available on wireless devices

The Google guys took Schmidt to task for some of his strategy decisions at Novell. Schmidt argued back. It was exactly the kind of intellectual duel that Brin and Page thrived on. By the time Schmidt left, the founders realized that they actually liked him. They called him later to discuss his interest in the company, and their interest in him. "We don't need you now," Page said, "but we think we're going to need you in the future."

The future came quickly. In August 2001, Schmidt became CEO and chairman of the company. His job would be to play the role of disciplinarian in Google's young, creative environment. He was amazed to find that the company was still using small-business software solutions for financial record-keeping and payroll systems and quickly implemented a system better suited to a company making millions of dollars.

Occasionally, Schmidt's business sense conflicted with the ambition of Brin and Page—most notably when the pair was on the verge of inking a deal as the official search engine of Internet giant America Online (AOL). AOL was asking for a huge financial guarantee from Google, as well as stock options. Although Brin and Page were willing to pay any price for the business, Schmidt wanted them to approach the deal more conservatively. The founders pulled rank on their CEO, however, and confidently completed the deal.

On May 1, 2002, AOL's 34 million subscribers found a small search box on every page that said, "Search Powered by Google." Soon, Google had also signed a deal to provide searches for the Internet provider Earthlink. Next came a three-year, $100-million deal to provide rival search engine Ask Jeeves with its text-based advertising. By the end of 2002, Google's balance sheet reflected $440 million in sales and $100 million in profits. Schmidt had to admit that Brin and Page had been right to pursue those partnerships. "They were more willing to take risk than me," he said. "They turned out to be right."

Brin and Page put much of the money that was coming in back into innovative ideas for expanding the search business—many of which came from the

An experienced corporate leader, Eric Schmidt helped Google truly take off after being hired as CEO in 2001

company's own employees. Google News, which offered free access to more than 4,500 news sources worldwide, was launched in September 2002. Froogle, a product search service, went online in test mode for the holiday shopping season a few months later. Google went global by making the site searchable in hundreds of languages, from Greek and Chinese to Russian and Danish and even a few "just for fun" tongues—Pig Latin and Klingon, for example.

As Google's product was improving, its appeal to advertisers was growing. So was its AdSense program, which offered other Web sites the technology to generate revenue by selling targeted ads that could be placed adjacent to their content. Of course, each site that bought the technology sent money to Google. The company was growing so fast and gaining so much positive attention that it had caught the eye of software giant Microsoft, which was reeling from a lawsuit claiming it had sought to establish a monopoly with its computer operating system. Google's success made Microsoft nervous about losing its position of dominance in the software industry. Although the two companies didn't compete head-to-head, they would both try to outdo the other with innovations and new ideas from that point on.

As 2003 came to an end, Google's site index had grown to include 4.28 billion Web pages. The company was being lauded in the press—it had been named "Brand of the Year" by Brandchannel, and Page and Brin had been named "Persons of the Week" by ABC News—and praised by users. As the company celebrated its fifth birthday, it seemed that things couldn't possibly get any better.

FEBRUARY 20, 2006

www.time.com AOL Keyword: TIME

WHO'S BEHIND THE CARTOON MAYHEM? ■ BEING OBAMA

TIME

Google honchos,
from top,
Larry Page,
Eric Schmidt and
Sergey Brin

RUST

SECRETS?

An exclusive inside look
at the $100 billion empire
that is dominating
the Internet

BY ADI IGNATIUS

> "Google's growth shows no sign of slowing.
> Despite capturing the majority of searches
> in the U.S., and in light of competitors'
> improvements, Google's market share of
> executed searches continues to grow...."
>
> BILL TANCER, RESEARCH MANAGER AT
> HITWISE, AN INTERNET METRICS FIRM

By 2003, Google's "big three" of Page, Brin, and Schmidt were being featured in major journals

GOOGLE

Every week, the software engineers at Google are encouraged to set aside their pressing projects for one day and focus on creative ideas of their own instead. It's known as the 20 percent rule, and it's helped launch several of Google's best-known products and services. Google News, for example, came out of an employee's efforts to organize news reports in the aftermath of the 9/11 terror attacks; Froogle, Google's shopping site, was developed by an engineer who spent his 20 percent time studying product searches. Another engineer created "Google 101," a seminar to better prepare students for computer careers. Even Gmail, Google's free Webmail service, came out of a 20 percent time project. Not every 20 percent time project comes to fruition, but CEO Eric Schmidt says the company relies on the ideas for innovation. "Virtually everything new seems to come from the 20 percent time," Schmidt says. "They certainly don't come from the management team."

CHAPTER FOUR

Searching the Stock Market

Although business was booming in 2004, Larry Page and Sergey Brin were convinced that they could do better. In particular, they were convinced that they could do e-mail better than such competitors as Microsoft, Yahoo!, and America Online. They wanted their version to be cheaper, easier to use, and superior in every other way to the other brands.

When Page and Brin announced the launch of Gmail with a press release on April 1, 2004, they expected lots of buzz. They were, after all, offering a greater amount of online storage space—a full **gigabyte**—to all subscribers, which was still unheard of in the industry. Even better, there was no cost at all for users. But the buzz that came out of their announcement was focused almost entirely on an aspect to which they hadn't given much thought: the fact that Google intended to run targeted ads in the e-mails. Privacy advocates were furious that the content of e-mails sent and received would be scanned to find keywords that could be paired with ads. Lawmakers threatened legislation. For the first time, Google's "good boy" image had been tarnished in a very public way.

"Google is risking its reputation for honesty and putting the user first with its new e-mail service," Walt Mossberg, a technology columnist for the *Wall Street*

Like Google, Yahoo! was founded by two Stanford graduate students (Jerry Yang and David Filo)

Journal, wrote. "The problem here isn't confusion between ads and editorial content. It's that Google is scanning your private e-mail to locate the keywords that generate the ads. This seems like an invasion of privacy."

Brin and Page were completely unprepared for the negative reaction to their Gmail announcement. They were convinced that the uproar would blow over once users had a chance to experience the product, but they still consulted a lawyer, who advised them to take steps to make searching e-mail archives impossible and to strip personal information about users from their records. They did not, however, change their plans to run ads with the e-mails.

The furor over Gmail was still raging when, on April 29, 2004, Google filed with the Securities and Exchange Commission (SEC) for an **initial public offering** (IPO). Although Page and Brin weren't eager to give up the freedom of private ownership, they knew it was time to reward the employees they had recruited with promises of stock options. They also knew that their investors—from the venture capital firms and Andy Bechtolsheim to the friends and family who had helped raise early funds—deserved to cash in on their investments. And they knew that an infusion of cash would allow their company to maintain its growth and achieve new things. But, as usual, it wasn't their style to go about the process in the conventional manner.

Their first move was to set the amount of money they hoped to raise through the IPO at $2,718,281,828.46—a numerical figure known as "constant e." They also refused to limit the number of investment houses guaranteeing the sale of the stock, which most companies do. And then they decided to set the price of Google's shares through an unusual and relatively unknown Dutch auction process, which allowed investors to bid for the shares online.

In the months between that announcement and the actual IPO, Google again faced fire from the media, industry analysts, and Wall Street observers, who thought the company was pricing its stock too high (the original forecast was for a range between $108 and $135 a share) and that it was being careless

> "We're not anywhere near done with search technology. [The year] 2010 or 2020 will make today look really sad."
>
> GOOGLE ENGINEER MARISSA MAYER

Google's comfortable offices in Mountain View, California, were designed to encourage creativity

with the rules for stock offerings. Some traditional businesspeople even considered Brin and Page to be arrogant and immature because they were doing things differently than usual.

But the worst was yet to come. During what is known as the "quiet period," in which the SEC requires a company issuing stock to refrain from any promotional publicity, Page and Brin were featured in a lengthy article in *Playboy* magazine. The interview had taken place in early April, before the company had even announced that it would be going public. The timing of its publication, however, was problematic. But Google's lawyers offered a possible solution: file the *Playboy* article as an **appendix** to the company's SEC registration statement, making it part of the official materials available to all investors. The plan worked. Although the SEC reserved the right to further investigate the matter at a later date, it allowed the IPO to go forward.

All the attention came to a head on August 19, 2004, when Google began trading on NASDAQ for $85 a share. Page went to Wall Street for the occasion, but Brin stayed in California to shepherd the day-to-day operations of the company. By the end of the day, both men were multimillionaires. Their company had raised $1.67 billion—short of their announced expectations, but still among the largest totals ever raised by a technology company.

In the wake of Google's IPO, Sergey Brin, Larry Page, and CEO Eric Schmidt all offered to take pay cuts. Brin and Page had been earning $150,000 annually, and Schmidt $250,000. But after each took home millions of dollars from the stock offering, they reduced their salaries to $1 a year.

Google's IPO in August 2004 instantly turned many of the company's employees into millionaires

A GOOGLER'S WORKDAY

Free food. A swimming pool, climbing wall, and pool tables. Laundry facilities (with free detergent) on-site. That's just the beginning of the benefits that Google offers to its more than 6,500 employees, from software engineers to secretaries. There's also the on-site beauty salon, doctor's office, and spa (all free). Working parents can bring their children to the free child-care center at the company's headquarters in Mountain View, California. Dogs are welcome. Employees are even given access to motorized scooters to travel around the sprawling Googleplex. And every now and then it's pajama day. Cofounders Larry Page and Sergey Brin have gone to such lengths to keep their employees happy that their company was named the "Best Company to Work For" by *Fortune Magazine* in 2007. "Work is such a cozy place that it's sometimes difficult for Google employees to leave the office," writer Adam Lashinsky said in the article, "which is precisely how the company justifies the expenses."

CHAPTER FIVE

Engines Roaring

G oogle held its first annual meeting for **shareholders** on May 12, 2005. The few hundred shareholders who showed up at the Googleplex, the name for company headquarters, for the meeting were treated to lunch, followed by "snicker-Google" cookies, the company's spin on the more familiar snickerdoodles.

Although they didn't get a comprehensive tour of the headquarters—any one of the attendees could have been from a competitor—they did get good news: The company's stock had soared past $225. Profits for the first three months of the year were at $369.3 million, with sales topping $1.3 billion. By the Fourth of July, Google's stock had broken the $300 mark, an unprecedented high for technology stocks.

The good news continued all year long, as Google developed new products, such as Google Maps, a directions and locations search, and Google Earth, which allowed users to view satellite images, maps, and three-dimensional images of sites around the world, down to buildings, objects such as cars, and sometimes even people. The company also expanded internationally, extending its agreement with America Online to provide search and advertising technology to AOL Europe, gaining exposure to approximately 6.3 million

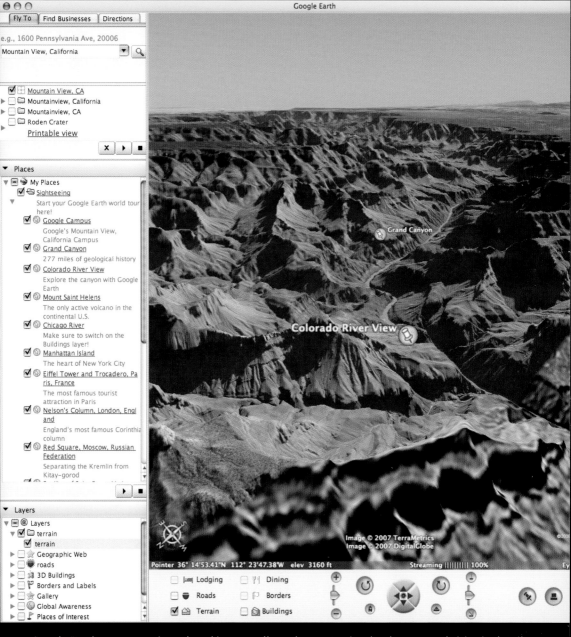

Google Earth, a program introduced in 2005, allowed users to view landscapes and cities in detail

people. It opened a European headquarters in Dublin,Ireland, a research and development center in Beijing, China, and offices in both Sao Paulo, Brazil, and Mexico City, Mexico.

Near the end of the year, Google renamed one of its most ambitious projects to date: Google Print became Google Book Search, a collection of online books from some of the world's largest and most prestigious libraries that had been scanned as part of Google's digitization project. The project had started in 2002, when Page approached his alma mater, the University of Michigan, with an of-fer to pay to have every book in the school's library scanned if he could add all the information to Google's index. He and Brin floated similar proposals at Stanford, Harvard, the New York Public Library, and others.

Even as they made those offers, they had no idea how long it would take to photograph each page so that it could be digitally scanned. Page and Marissa Mayer, Google's director of consumer Web products, started experimenting with the process. "We had a metronome to keep us on rhythm for turning the pages," Mayer said. "Larry's job was to click the shutter, and my job was to turn the pages. It took us about 45 minutes to do a 300-page book."

That was encouraging enough for the Google team to continue. Although the idea drew controversy over **copyright infringement** from some author groups, the company was willing to commit time and resources over the long term to the ongoing digitization project. "Maybe inside of 10 years we'll have all the knowledge that's ever been published in book form available and searchable online," Mayer said. "It's really a grand vision."

Google pursued the ideas of others almost as eagerly as it pursued its own. The company had already made several key acquisitions in its short history, each one adding another dimension to its own offerings. It bought Pyra Labs, which brought a **blogging** presence to Google. It acquired Upstartle, which brought an online word processing and spreadsheet component to the busi-ness. And in October 2006, Google paid $1.65 billion in stock to buy YouTube, a

By 2007, Google Book Search included more than a million digitized books and was scanning another 3,000 a day

popular online video site. "The YouTube team has built an exciting and powerful media platform that complements Google's mission to organize the world's information and make it universally accessible and useful," said Eric Schmidt. "Our companies share similar values; we both always put our users first and are committed to innovating to improve their experience."

Google was growing bigger and bigger, and its renown was reaching farther and farther. By the end of 2006, it was far and away the most used search engine on the Web, with a **market share** of more than 50 percent. Its closest competitor, Yahoo!, which had at one time used Google technology, claimed just 23 percent. The company's name had become synonymous with "search" and had even been added to the dictionary as a verb.

Such dominance led industry experts to wonder if another company could ever surpass Google as the leader in search technology. "It's inevitable," said Erik Hansen, the president of SiteSpect, a provider of search engine marketing and Web optimization technology, in 2007. "Google cannot stay on top forever. Yes, it is in the spotlight now, but a lot of smart and well-funded companies are developing technology that is different from what Google offers."

Such speculation only pushes the "googlers" at the Googleplex to work toward the next best thing—from searching television services and offering on-air advertising plans to voice-activated phone directory searches, mobile phone services, and any number of other as-yet undisclosed plans. "We don't talk much about what lies ahead," the company reported on its Web site, "because we believe one of our chief competitive advantages is surprise."

In the past decade, Google has offered its users one surprise after another. The company may have been founded on a dream and a shoestring budget, but in fewer than 10 years, it has become one of the most profitable businesses in the world. Considering the dedication of Google's two young founders, that really isn't such a surprise. "I think we all feel a tremendous amount of responsibility for getting many, many people in the world their information," Larry Page said.

> "I think [Google] is the smallest of accomplishments that we hope to make over the next 25 years. But I think that if Google is all we create, I don't think I would be very disappointed."
>
> GOOGLE COFOUNDER SERGEY BRIN

By 2007, plans were in motion for Google to team with NASA to post space mission information online

Larry Page (left) and Sergey Brin

Company lore insists that Larry Page and Sergey Brin didn't particularly like each other when they met as PhD students on the Stanford campus in 1995. They were known to challenge each other constantly and to argue often over silly ideas (including, as one fellow student recalled, whether it was possible to construct a building-size display out of lima beans). But the two have been nearly inseparable since that time. They were so frequently seen together on campus that their names eventually became one—"LarryandSergey." Soon, so did their academic pursuits. By mid-1996, Page and Brin, who shared office space in Stanford's William Gates Science Center, were working together to download and analyze Web links. Two years later, they had turned that idea into the Google search engine. Today, they continue to be almost constant companions—and they still share an office (albeit a much more spacious one) at the sprawling Googleplex.

GLOSSARY

appendix a collection of supplementary material that is attached to documentation to help explain or clarify other materials

blogging contributing regularly to an ongoing personal journal about a specified topic on the World Wide Web

board of directors a group of people in charge of making big decisions for a publicly owned company

copyright infringement a violation of rights in which one person or company benefits by using the work or ideas of another person or company illegally

doctoral thesis a written paper based on research examining a new idea or point of view, especially as a requirement for an advanced academic degree

executive a decision-making leader of a company, such as the president or chief executive officer (CEO)

gigabyte a unit of computer memory or data storage capacity equal to 1,024 megabytes, or one billion bytes (computer hard drives often have 160 or more gigabytes)

hard drives computer parts that read and write data, or information, on computer disks

hardware computers and the associated physical equipment directly involved in processing data

incorporated forming a firm or company into a corporation by completing all of the required procedures and paperwork

initial public offering the first sale of stock by a company to the public; it is generally done to raise funds for the company, which is then owned by investors rather than an individual or group of individuals

links a segment of text or a graphical item that serves as a cross-reference between parts of a Web-based document or between different Web pages

market share the percentage of the total sales of a given type of product or service that are attributable to a particular company

merger the combining of two or more entities into one through a purchase or a pooling of interests

NASDAQ an acronym for the National Association of Securities Dealers Automated Quotation system; it is a computerized system used to trade shares in public companies

quarter one of four three-month intervals that together comprise the financial year; public companies must report certain data on a quarterly basis

search engine a Web site whose primary function is locating information available on the Internet or a portion of the Internet

shareholders people or corporations who own shares of stock (portions of ownership) in a corporation

start-ups new business ventures in their earliest stage of development

stock options options for employees or investors in a company to buy or sell that company's stock; stock options are often given as part of an employee's benefits package

venture capital funds made available to small businesses that are starting out but show great potential for growth

SELECTED BIBLIOGRAPHY

Basch, Reva. "The Saga as Google Goes Public." *Searcher* 13, no. 1 (2005): 18–28.

Battelle, John. *The Search: How Google and Its Rivals Rewrote the Rules of Business and Transformed Our Culture.* New York: Portfolio Trade, 2006.

LaGesse, David. "Engine of Fun and Profit." *U.S. News & World Report* 139, no. 16 (2005): 16.

Sherman, Chris. *Google Power: Unleash the Full Potential of Google.* New York: McGraw-Hill, 2005.

Vise, David A., and Mark Malseed. *The Google Story.* New York: Bantam Dell, 2005.

INDEX